CALLING

SEPARATION

BOB YANDIAN

 Whitaker House

CALLING & SEPARATION

Bob Yandian
Bob Yandian Ministries
P.O. Box 55236
Tulsa, OK 74155

ISBN: 0-88368-353-9
Printed in the United States of America
Copyright © 1991 by Bob Yandian

Whitaker House
580 Pittsburgh Street
Springdale, PA 15144

2 3 4 5 6 7 8 9 10 11 12 / 04 03 02 01 00 99 98 97 96 95

Dedication

To Kirby Andersen, my former associate pastor, who exemplifies faithfulness like no other I know.

Contents

Introduction

Have you ever wondered why some Christians, who are obviously called and anointed by God for ministry, never seem to move into the realm of success? We watch and wonder as they struggle with frustration, knocking on doors that never open, while others step easily into pulpits and have opportunities knocking at their door. One minister prays for any speaking engagement, while another prays over stacks of invitations, seeking God's will for which ones he should accept. Why are so many called, but so few chosen?

Maybe you are in this same situation. You know that a call of God is in your heart, but you don't know where to begin.

7

Perhaps you are putting all of your plans and decisions about ministry on hold, thinking a tremendous door, *the* door to success, might open tomorrow. After all, how can you teach children's church or be an usher today when Africa could open up tomorrow? So you sit, week after week, month after month, year after year, watching as others are ordained and sent to the ends of the earth. If you weren't afraid of committing the sin of blasphemy, you might blame God for being a respecter of persons!

As you already know, God is not your problem, He is your answer. He has placed in your heart a supernatural key ring that holds every key you need for success in life. So, how do you discover these keys?

> *³ According as His divine power hath given unto us all things [the keys] that pertain unto life and godliness, **through the knowledge of him** that hath called us to glory and virtue.*
> *⁴ Whereby are given unto us exceeding great and precious **promises**.*
> (2 Peter 1:3-4)

In His Word, God gives us the *"keys of the kingdom of heaven"* (Matthew 16:19). Now, I want you to notice that Jesus never told us He would give us the "key," but the *"keys"* to the kingdom. A mistake that we often make is to assume that one key, or one monumental revelation, will radically change our whole life and set us on the fast track of powerful ministry and successful living forever.

Browsing through Christian magazines, books, and tapes, you will many times see the phrase, "the key to successful ministry." In reality, there are a handful of significant keys of understanding and wisdom which are revealed to us as we study, meditate, and act on the Word of God. These keys unlock secrets of success and give us insights which become major mile markers in our walk with the Lord. Some of these are the grace of God, our right standing before God, the authority of the believer, and the subject of this book— *calling and separation*.

It's time to open your heart and pull out your key ring! You are going to be

given a key from God's Word to help you
fulfill your ministry. It is a key that will
surely change your thinking about ministry and redirect your life. Instead of seeing
God from your perspective, you will see
yourself from His, by the mirror of His
Word. You can know what He is expecting
from your life and begin to fulfill His will
today.

Then, when the door to your ultimate
ministry opens up before you, you will be
ready. You will step through the door not
by your own devices, but in the confidence
of His wisdom, knowing that you are *"His
workmanship, created in Christ Jesus unto
good works, which God hath before ordained that we should walk in them"*
(Ephesians 2:10).

One

Calling & Separation Defined

Paul, a servant of Jesus Christ, called to be an apostle, separated unto the gospel of God.
—Romans 1:1

In this first verse of Romans, Paul declares the two-fold aspect of ministry: *calling and separation*. Because the New Testament tells us that Paul and the other apostles are our examples, if we can understand Paul's calling and separation

into the ministry, then we can understand
our own.

The apostles were no better than we
are, nor did they operate by a different set
of rules than we do today. In 2 Thessalo-
nians 3:9, Paul said that he had made
himself an example for us to follow. Although we may not stand in the offices
that he stood in, the keys that made him a
successful minister are the same keys that
will make us successful ministers.

> [15] *But when it pleased God, who sepa-*
> *rated me from my mother's womb,*
> *and called me by his grace.*
>   (Galatians 1:15)

This verse says that both our calling
and our separation are by the grace of
God. Obviously, if they were given to Paul
while he was in his mother's womb, how
could he work for, earn, or deserve them?

Ephesians 1:3-14 says that God had a
plan for your life from before the foundation of the world. You are so special that
He mapped out a course for you before you

ever existed. Therefore, you can see that both your calling and separation are given by grace, because you weren't around before the foundation of the world to do anything to earn them!

> *18 But now hath God set the members every one of them in the body, as it hath pleased him.*
>
>   (1 Corinthians 12:18)

> *7 But unto every* [each] *one of us is given grace according to the measure of the gift of Christ.*   (Ephesians 4:7)

What is a "Calling"?

Paul was *"called"* to be an apostle (Romans 1:1), and the Greek word for called comes from the root word *kaleo,* which means to call aloud, to summon, or call toward.

If you have been born again, you have a calling, because a calling is simply the will of God for your life. It is the work God wants you to accomplish during the time you are on earth.

Every believer has a calling on his or her life, but whether or not that calling is fulfilled depends on several factors. First, we must recognize the call, and second, we must accept it.

To recognize the calling, or to know the will of God for your life, you begin with prayer. Ask God to show you the purpose and plan for your life.

When you know your calling, one of the most important prayers you pray in the Christian life is the prayer of consecration and dedication. This is when you open your heart to God and become willing to do whatever He asks.

> [1] *I therefore, the prisoner of the Lord, beseech you that ye walk worthy of the vocation wherewith ye are called.*
>   (Ephesians 4:1)

This verse refers to our calling as our "*vocation.*" Just as there are natural vocations such as carpenters, businessmen, salesmen, or school teachers, there are spiritual vocations. When we are born again, our spiritual vocation may or may not be compatible with our natural vocation.

For instance, some believers are called to work at an office, factory, or school and to be witnesses through these vocations. But others are called to leave a natural vocation because their spiritual vocation is a full-time position, such as pastor, evangelist, or missionary.

Whether we are called to be witnesses in a natural vocation or are called to full-time ministry, we can only have the supernatural peace of God when we accept His will for our lives and stop trying to force our will on Him. We can never be happy by putting ourselves into a ministry or a natural vocation by our own will. But when we seek and accept our calling from God, then our lives become fuller and richer than we ever dreamed possible.

What Does Being "Separated" Mean?

The word we translate "separate" in the original Greek is *aphorao*, which means to set apart by boundaries, or to sever. It has the dual meaning of separating someone *from* something, while separating them *to* something.

The period of time from when we are called until our point of separation may be short or long. The calling can be recognized and accepted, but separation, or the fulfilling of that call, has not yet arrived.

For example, a man gets saved while he is working as a carpenter. Shortly after that the Holy Spirit reveals to him that he is called to the mission field. He accepts the call, but has no peace about quitting his job.

This missionary may drive nails and saw boards for many months or even years before the mission door opens up. However, when he feels released to leave his job, God is separating him from his carpentry position to the mission field.

Later on, while he is serving as a missionary, God may speak to his heart that he will pastor a church someday. The call on his life is becoming more refined, but he continues on the mission field. Again, even though he has accepted the call to pastor, God has not yet separated him to the pulpit.

One day, as he speaks at a certain church, he senses that this is where he will pastor. Through a series of events, he is asked to take the position. God then separates him from the mission field to the office of pastor.

An important point to mention here is that God has a calling and a point of separation for every believer, whether they submit to His will for their lives or not. I believe many Christians are miserable and will die frustrated because they never sought God for or accepted the calling and/or separation He had for them. This is very sad.

God knows of our calling and separation in His foreknowledge. Revelation comes to us when we recognize and accept what God has known from eternity past. He has already set our course, and He is waiting for us to choose to follow it. Therefore, we must conclude that He is waiting on us, rather than it being we who are waiting on Him.

From Damascus To Antioch

God had a calling for the Apostle Paul in his mother's womb (Galatians 1:15). However, before that calling could be fulfilled, a series of events had to take place, and Paul had to make certain decisions.

First of all, since only a believer can be called, Paul had to accept Jesus as Lord. This occurred on the road to Damascus when Jesus spoke to him from a blinding light (see Acts 9). At that moment, Paul submitted to the call of God without knowing what it was. He asked, *"Lord, what wilt thou have me do?"* And when Jesus answered, *"Arise, and go into the city, and it shall be told thee what thou must do"* (v. 6), Paul obeyed.

God used a common believer named Ananias, who was mentioned only briefly in the Word of God, to reveal what Paul's calling was:

> *15 He is a chosen vessel unto me, to bear my name before the Gentiles, and kings, and the children of Israel:*

*16 for I will show him great things he
must suffer for my name's sake.*
                              (Acts 9:15-16)

God knew Paul's calling long before it
was revealed to Ananias or Paul, and He
also knew the point at which He would
separate Paul for the work of that calling.
But Paul's separation to the ministry occurred many years later.

More than fourteen years elapsed between the call on the road to Damascus
and the time when the Holy Spirit spoke
to Paul and Barnabas at the church in
Antioch:

*1 Now there were in the church that
was at Antioch certain prophets and
teachers; as Barnabas, and Simeon
that was called Niger, and Lucius of
Cyrene, and Manaen, which hat been
brought up with Herod the tetrarch,
and Saul.*
*2 As they ministered to the Lord, and
fasted, the Holy Ghost said, separate
me Barnabas and Saul for the work
whereunto I have called them.*
                              (Acts 13:1-2)

Notice the verb tenses used by the Holy Spirit in the second verse. *"Separate me"* is present tense, and *"have called"* is past tense. What we are seeing here, again, is that there is a period of time between the moment we are called to minister and the moment we are separated to do the work of that ministry.

Soon after Paul accepted Jesus as Lord on the road to Damascus, he experienced the urging of the Holy Spirit to leave his former lifestyle and to prepare himself for a ministry to the Gentiles. Although no doors for actual ministry opened for many years, Paul knew what God had called him to do.

What was it that brought Paul to the point where the Holy Spirit sovereignly and supernaturally opened the door and sent him out? This moment was so dramatic in Paul's life that it was marked by a supernatural manifestation of the Holy Spirit heard by all who were present (Acts 13:1-2). What happened in Paul's life during the fourteen years between Damascus and Antioch?

Many people recognize and accept a call to the ministry, but never reach the point of separation. Is there a key on our divine key ring that will show us the way from calling to separation?

Two

The Key of
Faithfulness

A ministerial student who was attending the church I pastor approached me one day and proudly informed me that God had called him to pastor. When I nodded and replied, "That's great," he repeated himself. I nodded again and replied again, "That's great." He seemed to be getting more agitated, so after he announced to me the third time that he was called to pastor, I bluntly asked him what he was getting at.

He told me that he wanted to preach from the pulpit of our church and asked if he would ever have that opportunity. I asked him to tell me where he was involved at the moment. Was he an usher, teaching a Sunday school class, greeting at the door, helping with clean-up, or serving communion? He said, "I'm called to pastor. Now that I know what my calling is, I don't want to do those other things."

"Well," I said, "you may be *called*, but you are not *separated* yet." At the rate he was going, it was doubtful that he would ever reach the point of separation. He would be one of the many who are called, but not one of the few who are chosen.

Between calling and separation, we find a tremendous key to the kingdom of God: *faithfulness*. Few will pay the price to become faithful and put their hand to the plow, to do whatever needs to be done at the place they find themselves at the moment. They are waiting for their golden opportunity to fall from heaven, for that mighty door of powerful ministry to swing wide open before them.

Although the point of separation comes from God, the timing is dependent upon us. Our calling is merely accepted; it demands no level of maturity on our part to know we are called and to acknowledge God's will for our lives. However, separation is a mark of maturity. This is the point where God knows He can trust us to handle the tasks associated with the call.

Therefore, the point of separation will never come if God's prerequisites are not met, and it can be forfeited by sin in the minister's life or apathy toward the will of God. Paul called this type of minister a *"shipwreck"* (1 Timothy 1:19) or a *"castaway"* (1 Corinthians 9:27).

Revelation in Arabia

In the first chapter of Galatians, Paul writes about the early days of his ministry and what he did to bring his calling to the point of separation:

> [15] *But when it pleased God, who separated me from my mother's womb, and called me by his grace,*

¹⁶ To reveal his Son in me, that I
might preach him among the heathen;
immediately, I conferred not with
flesh and blood:
¹⁷ Neither went I up to Jerusalem to
them which were apostles before me;
but I went into Arabia, and returned
again unto Damascus.
¹⁸ Then after three years I went up to
Jerusalem to see Peter, and abode
with him fifteen days.
¹⁹ But other of the apostles saw I none,
save James the Lord's brother.
²⁰ Now the things which I write unto
you, behold, before God, I lie not.
²¹ Afterwards I came unto the regions
of Syria and Cilicia;
²² And was unknown by face unto the
churches of Judea which were in
Christ:
²³ But they had heard only, that he
which persecuted us in times past now
preacheth the faith which once he destroyed.
²⁴ And they glorified God in me.
¹ Then fourteen years after I went up
again to Jerusalem with Barnabas,
and took Titus with me also.

(Galatians 1:15-2:1)

After Paul was saved on the road to Damascus, he obeyed the Lord's Word and went into Damascus to wait for Ananias to lay hands on him. It was during this time that the Holy Spirit revealed his calling. However, once he knew his calling, Paul did something very unusual. He left Damascus and went to Arabia, without consulting any of those who had actually walked with Jesus during His ministry on earth and after His death and resurrection.

Now the first thing most ministers would do, knowing that they had a calling, would be to go to Jerusalem and hang around with the other apostles. After all, Jerusalem was the place to be! The church there was pastored by James, the half-brother of the Lord Jesus, and every celebrity in the ministry would be there.

On any normal day you might see Peter and John sitting in church, and occasionally Matthew and Thomas might come through after a few months on the road. Certainly, if you knew you were called and you wanted doors of ministry to open to

you, the First Church of Jerusalem was
where you should go to be seen.

Why would anyone go to Arabia? No
one was in Arabia! But this is where God
told Paul to go, and He knew what He was
doing. This is where He trained Moses,
and this is where He would give Paul a
powerful and dynamic revelation of the
Lord Jesus Christ.

Before you can preach, you must know
what to preach, which is why revelation
always comes before preaching. Paul knew
he had to get a revelation of the Lord in
order to fulfill his calling. By going to Arabia, he moved toward that point of separation. He must have spent a lot of time in
prayer, fasting, and intensive study of the
Word, because when he returned to Damascus, he had received a fresh revelation
of Jesus for the body of Christ!

It's interesting to note that when Paul
left Arabia and returned to Damascus, he
still waited three years before visiting Jerusalem. And when he finally did go there,
he only stayed for fifteen days, seeing no
one but Peter and James. He didn't even

go to church! In the eyes of man, this is not the way to start a successful ministry.

He should have stopped by the church for at least one meeting in order to hand out a few of his cards to those who were visiting from other areas. He could have distributed a few of his cards to traveling ministers, encouraging them to tell pastors on the road that he was now "doing meetings." But instead, he left Jerusalem and did not return for fourteen years.

If Paul had walked down the streets of that great city, no one would have recognized him. However, the Bible tells us that even though his face was not known in "Ministry Mecca," news of his miraculous conversion was widespread.

Paul learned early to remain faithful to do whatever his hand found to do and let his reputation speak for itself. He did not use his testimony or his former life to open doors for his ministry. He knew the truth of this statement: If the Lord does not promote you, you are not promoted.

Paul knew that men may not know where he was located, but the Lord knew.

You do not need to be where success is located to be successful yourself. God will bring success to you as you are faithful.

The Tortoise Always Wins

I realized I had a call on my life when I was a junior at Oklahoma State University. I was miserable in my business administration major, so I decided to go to Bible school to find out whether or not this was really God.

In 1969 and 1970, I attended Trinity Bible School in Tulsa, Oklahoma. The school had only thirty-five students and was taught by Charles Duncombe, a Britisher who was an evangelistic associate of Smith Wigglesworth. I remember writing an essay on the first day of school that told of my desire to be a Bible teacher. At the time, I did not know that I would be a pastor one day, but I thought I would love teaching in a Bible school.

During the last days of school, many students were sending out applications and resumes to churches and mission works. By graduation, most of them had churches to go to or works to take over, but I had nothing. They would ask me what I was going to do, because it was obvious to them that I had a gift to teach and that I was *called*. I felt tremendous pressure to make something up or stretch the truth, but I decided not to. I told them I would teach a Sunday school class at the church I was attending, and then accept any speaking invitation I might get. Frankly, I felt like the race had started, the rabbits had taken off, and I was the tortoise!

In order to support my wife and myself, I took a job, and I continued to study the Bible in the evenings. I put together numerous sermons and teachings—with no place to teach them. If someone would have asked me to do a meeting, I could have stayed a month!

At my church, I began by teaching a class of junior high boys, then the college and career class. Not long after that, I helped another pastor begin Grace Fellowship, the church I now pastor, by setting

up the sound system and dubbing audio
cassette tapes.

All of this seemed to be getting me
nowhere, when I was asked to take a Sunday evening class of newly-marrieds and
singles. The group began with seven people, but I would study all week long for it.
In my spare time, I took a class in Greek
to help with my studying, and I came
"loaded for bear" every meeting.

The class loved it In the five years that
I taught that Sunday evening group, it
grew to over two hundred people! Unfor-
tunately, the room where we met could
only hold a little over a hundred!

One evening, the Dean of Instructors
at Rhema Bible Training Center sat in on
my class at church and heard me teach.
The next morning he called me into his
office, and I was hired as a part-time
teacher at Rhema. I thought I had died
and gone to heaven! I was actually getting
paid to teach the Word of God.

This was seven years after graduating
from Bible school and nine years after I
had felt and accepted the call of God into

the ministry. My point of separation had finally come.

Success came in waves after that. The next year I was made full-time instructor, and two years later I became the Dean of Instructors. Then, after four years of teaching at Rhema, God called me to pastor the church I had helped from its beginning, Grace Fellowship. Since 1980 when I became its pastor, the church has grown from 1,200 to over 3,000 members.

To be honest, I look at myself and wonder why God would use me. I do not have the education nor the ability to administrate that many ministers have. Basically, I am "the klutz that succeeded." But I found a key to success: *faithfulness pays off.*

Many of the students I went to Bible school with are not even in the ministry today. They tried to open their own doors or entered the ministry in their own strength, and they have fallen one by one. But, as you recall, the rabbit did not win the race; the tortoise did. Waiting on the Lord demands patience and faithfulness,

but He will bless the plodder and reward
him with supernatural wisdom and
strength.

> *[30] Even the youths shall faint and be
> weary, and the young men shall ut-
> terly fall:*
> *[31] But they that wait upon the Lord
> shall renew* [exchange] *their strength;
> they shall mount up with wings as
> eagles; they shall run, and not be
> weary; and they shall walk, and not
> faint.*   (Isaiah 40:30-31)

Three

The Rewards of Faithfulness

*As ye also learned of Epaphras our dear
fellow servant, who is for you* [on your
behalf] *a faithful minister of Christ.*
—*Colossians 1:7*

Until this time, you have probably never heard of Epaphras, who was the pastor of the church at Colosse. Paul mentions him as *"a faithful minister"* of the Gospel, which is the highest commendation he could give to any minister. You will also notice that the verse did not mention that Epaphras was responsible for a great home cell group program, Sunday school, or singles' ministry. Paul did not congratulate him for the number of members in attendance or great music ministry. All of these areas are emphasized by ministers today when they are looking for greatness in a church or pastor, and most church conferences seem to focus more on church growth instead of the integrity or character of the minister.

Epaphras, however, was not a well-known man of the New Testament. He was a plodder, and a plodder moves slowly. He doesn't get exasperated at the distance yet to go, but thanks God for each inch he has attained. He knows well that faithfulness moves slowly but surely, gaining inches a week instead of miles a minute.

A plodder doesn't get upset at the empty seats at each service, but rejoices over the ones that are full. He doesn't gripe to the ones who do come about the ones who do not come. He knows that if you thank the ones who come and feed them well on the Word of God, they will reach out and bring others to fill the empty seats!

Colossians 1:7 tells us that Epaphras was faithful, but what he was faithful to is mentioned later in that epistle:

> [12] *Epaphras, who is one of you, a servant of Christ, saluteth you, always laboring fervently for you in prayers, that ye may stand perfect [mature] and complete in all the will of God.*
>
> (Colossians 4:12)

Epaphras was faithful in two areas: ministry of the Word of God and prayer (also mentioned in Acts 6:4). This means that he taught his congregation the entire Word of God (not singling out pet doctrines), and then prayed for them to grow and become mature in the Word they had heard.

A subtle point must be mentioned here. The Holy Spirit does not say that Epaphras prayed for his sermons to be good. Many pastors do most of their praying for themselves, *before* the sermon. But

Epaphras did his praying for the congregation, **after** the sermon!

Proverbs 28:20 says that God blesses the faithful man: *"A faithful man shall abound with blessings."* He does not try to promote himself, but remains faithful to do what he is called to do. Faithfulness will not only bring rewards for him on this earth, but also for eternity:

> [23] *...Well done good and faithful servant; thou hast been faithful over a few things, I will make thee ruler over many things: enter thou into the joy of the Lord.*   (Matthew 25:23)

Greatness Begins at the Bottom

No one in the business world *or* the church begins at the top. Faithfulness is proven at the bottom, as we work for someone else. How can you expect to rule over much when you will not be faithful over the little things now? How will you be prepared to stand behind the pulpit to minister the Word to the people, when you will not greet them at the door, usher them to their seats, teach their children in Sunday school, or serve them communion?

We may not like the way the pastor runs the church, the Sunday school superintendent handles the classes, or the choir director leads the choir, but God still leads us to put our hand to the plow and submit to the leadership in the areas to which He calls us.

If you are looking for a perfect church with a perfect pastor, staff, and workers, you will have to die and go to heaven to find it! God calls *imperfect people* into the ministry, and we are all treasures in *earthen vessels*. The fact of the matter is, the faster you learn to submit to an imperfect pastor, youth director, or music director, the more the Lord loves it, and the faster He will promote you and bring you to the time for your separation.

Being faithful around difficult people improves your character. This is where you *"work out your own salvation with fear and trembling!"* (Philippians 2:12). The fruit of the Spirit must come forth in

your life to establish a solid foundation of
unshakable faith and integrity under
whatever gifts and calling God has given
you. And I will add that many of the people I have worked for and ministered with
before I became a pastor taught me more
what *not to do* than what to do!

Who Are the Stars?

> ² *And the things that thou hast heart
> of* [from] *me among many witnesses,
> the same commit* [deposit] *thou to
> faithful men, who shall be able to
> teach others also.*   (2 Timothy 2:2)

When a pastor looks for someone in
the congregation to use in a special capac-
ity, what characteristic do you think the
Word of God instructs him to look for?

Paul's final words of wisdom and in-
struction before his death are contained in
Second Timothy where he turned many of
his responsibilities over to one of his favor-
ite ministers and friends, Timothy. In the
verse above, Paul reminds Timothy of

something very important that he must have witnessed in Paul's ministry for years: Paul found faithful men and taught them how to be the teachers and preachers they needed to be in order to fulfill their calling and minister to the people.

When Paul found these men, they were not always qualified to teach or preach, but they *were faithful*. Paul found Timothy on his second missionary journey, and Timothy was one of these faithful men. Acts 16:1-2 tells us that he had a great reputation for dependability and commitment to the things of God.

In 2 Timothy, however, now that Timothy is pastoring, he has forgotten about the importance of faithfulness and dependability. Somehow the rules have changed since *he* first started out in the ministry. Now he is looking for the "whiz kids" in the audience, those who can "preach heaven down," and he is overlooking the faithful men and women who surround him each day.

Let's look at this verse again. *"And the things that thou hast heard of me among many witnesses, the same commit thou to faithful men, who* **shall be able** *to teach others also."* When Paul found them, they were faithful, but not qualified. *"Faithful"* is in the sense of the present, and *"shall be able to teach"* is in future tense.

Timothy, like most pastors, probably shuttered at this command, because the faithful people are usually the jerks, the flakes. They have a big smile, carry a huge Bible under their arm, and butcher the Scriptures when they quote them. They come early, stay late, and are usually in the pastor's face after each service asking dumb questions anyone should be able to figure out.

They volunteer for anything and everything. Usually they have the rest of the congregation and the deacons sighing and rolling their eyes when they do, because everyone knows they are all zeal and no knowledge.

But let me jog your memory like Paul did Timothy's: What were you like when you were first saved and when you first knew you had a calling into some sort of ministry? Did God call you into the ministry because of your tremendous abilities and talents, or did He put you there because you were a faithful dolt, too?

Did you bug other ministers around you with unending questions and offers to help in anything that even remotely needed attention? Do you think everyone looked forward to your presence, or did they often wish you weren't such a pest? We should always put ourselves in remembrance of this Scripture:

> *26 For ye see your calling, brethren, how that not many wise men after the flesh, not many mighty, not many noble, are called:*
> *27 But God hath chosen the foolish things of the weak to confound the wise; and God hath chosen the weak things of the world to confound the things which are mighty.*
>
> (1 Corinthians 1:26-27)

No matter how flaky or immature we begin, if we are faithful, God will always reward our faithfulness with promotion.

When a person is faithful to do whatever his hand finds to do, the Word of God says:

> [6] *Humble yourselves therefore under the mighty hand of God, that he may exalt you in due season.*
>
> (1 Peter 5:6)

and

> [13] *For they that have used the office of a deacon well purchase to themselves a good degree* [promotion].
>
> (1 Timothy 3:13)

Four

Qualifications *vs.* Faithfulness

Well done, thou good and faithful servant;
thou hast been faithful over a few things, I
will make thee ruler over many things.
        —Matthew 25:23

After I became pastor of Grace Fellowship, one of my greatest desires was to incorporate a bookstore within the church, so we began this effort on a small scale. I asked the audio director to set up a table in the corner of the auditorium to sell tapes of the services.

As this ministry took off, books and other materials were sold as well as tapes. It soon became such a large part of the church that the audio director was handling two full-time jobs. We needed to find someone to take over the bookstore. My first thought was, What *qualifications* are required to run this new department?

There was a girl who worked in the audio department as a volunteer who was always faithful to her position. Her name came up a time or two, but we always disregarded her because she was not qualified. The position called for someone who knew accounting, bookkeeping, and inventory procedures, someone who could talk to book distributors and publishers.

The audio director and I made a list of everyone in the congregation we knew who even came close to having these qualifications and then asked them to pray about the position. Everyone on our list said the same thing: they appreciated the offer but did not feel they could take it. We were frustrated, and all we knew to do was to wait on God to supply the right person.

Every Saturday I prayed over the seats in the auditorium, asking God for the hearts of the people to be open to receive the Word of God, and for the gifts of the Holy Spirit to be in manifestation. On one particular Saturday, I did not know that while I was praying, the girl who volunteered in the audio department was upstairs in the booth setting volume controls and threading tape decks for the services.

As I prayed, she came downstairs to set up the microphones on the platform. When she got to the bottom of the steps, I caught a glimpse of her out of the corner of my eye, and a Scripture rose inside me:

> ² *Moreover* [most of all] *it is required in a steward, that a man be found faithful.*   (1 Corinthians 4:2)

At that moment, the Lord taught me some things that I have never forgotten. I had been looking for **qualifications**, but He looks for **faithfulness**. He said that you can teach a person qualifications, but you cannot teach them faithfulness. They must choose it for themselves, apart from any coercion of others. Suddenly, I understood what He was teaching me.

God did not put me in the ministry because of my great qualifications. I had been faithful to teach Sunday school classes, put up and tear down audio equipment, and volunteer for anything I could find for years. My qualifications had come as I was faithful to do whatever God and those I was serving at the time asked of me. I was faithful before I was qualified.

I stared at the girl set up the microphones. This was a weekly activity for her. She was not only faithful during each service, but also on weekdays when no one else was around. It takes great faith to work when no one but the Lord sees you.

Needless to say, this faithful girl was hired for the job, and we sent her to classes and other bookstores to receive the qualifications she needed.

> [11] *And I saw heaven opened, and behold a white horse; and he that sat upon him was called Faithful and True.* (Revelation 19:11)

> [23] *Great is thy faithfulness!*
> (Lamentations 3:23)

> [23] *He is faithful that promised.*
> (Hebrews 10:23)

One of God's greatest attributes is His faithfulness. Our Father is called faithful many times in the Word of God, and Jesus Christ is called Faithful before He is called True! His highest attribute is faithfulness.

I also want you to notice that in Matthew 25:23, the Lord did not say, "Well done, good and *qualified* servant." Our Lord rewards us in this life and through eternity according to our faithfulness, not our abilities.

Now, I am not saying that qualifications are bad, or that qualified people are automatically eliminated from consideration for positions in the church or business. But qualifications and abilities must be built on a foundation of faithfulness.

If a person depends on his qualifications, he will become arrogant and develop a condescending attitude toward others when he is successful. Likewise, he will become depressed and fearful when he fails. He is consumed with himself and his achievements, and is most likely using the position as a stepping stone to something greater—always looking out the window for his "big break" to come along. Everything he does is to enhance his resume, and though his abilities may be great, his character and integrity are sadly lacking.

On the other hand, a faithful person is a great treasure, a diamond in the rough. He is sold out to God, the church, and the pastor. He believes that his church is the best in the world. He will stick with the job come hell or high water! He considers it the highest honor to be paid to work there, and if it's God's will, he will work there until Jesus comes! In the beginning he may require a lot of work and patience, but the rewards of his longevity and dependability make him worth it.

> [6] *Most men will proclaim every one his own goodness: but a faithful man who can find?*   (Proverbs 20:6)

Five

God Defends the Faithful

Moses had been a single man for quite some time after his first wife, Zipporah, had left him at a roadside inn on the way to Egypt (Exodus 4:19-26). At one time his father-in-law, Jethro, had tried to get them back together (Exodus 18:1-7), but it didn't work.

Since the time of Zipporah's departure, Moses' sister Miriam had stood by him and had taken an active part in the daily decision-making processes and challenges of governing the nation of Israel. So when Moses decided to take a new wife, Miriam felt threatened about her position.

As soon as Miriam felt the competition of a new woman on the scene, she needed someone to fight her cause with her, and Aaron was the obvious choice. He was easily persuaded and apparently a wimp. Remember that it was he who allowed the people to build a golden calf when Moses was on Mount Sinai with God, and he even went so far as to help build an altar for worship and sacrifice to another god (Exodus 32:1-6).

> [1] *Miriam and Aaron spake against Moses because of the Ethiopian woman whom he had married: for he had married an Ethiopian woman.*
> [2] *And they said, Hath the Lord indeed spoken only by Moses? hath he not spoken also by us? and the Lord heard it.*   (Numbers 12:1-2)

Notice what Miriam and Aaron said to each other: "*Hath the Lord indeed spoken **only** by Moses?* Why can't we have as much say in the running of this nation as he does? We can hear from the Lord as well as he can.

They do not mention God sending down fire at *their* command, or splitting the Red Sea with their rods. They did not say that God told *them* which rock to strike or which tree to cut down to provide water for the people. It wasn't them who arranged with God for the daily provision of manna or quail. And they were not the ones who met every day with the Lord in the tabernacle.

Nevertheless, Miriam felt insecure and spoke to Aaron out of jealousy. Though they thought that they were talking in secret, the Word of God says that *"the Lord heard it."*

God did not waste any time bringing the issue to a head! The Lord spoke immediately to Moses, Miriam, and Aaron. He chose to do so before the entire nation, in front of the tabernacle where He met with Moses each day. He would personally settle the dispute over who was to govern Israel.

[3] *(Now the man Moses was very meek, above all the men which were upon the face of the earth.)*

*⁴ And the Lord spake suddenly unto
Moses, and unto Aaron, and unto
Miriam, Come out ye three unto the
tabernacle of the congregation. And
they three came out.*
*⁵ And the Lord came town in the pil-
lar of the cloud, and stood in the door
of the tabernacle, and called Aaron
and Miriam: and they both came forth.*
*⁶ And he said, Hear now my words. If
there be a prophet among you, I the
Lord will make myself known unto
him in a vision, and will speak unto
him in a dream.*   (Numbers 12:3-6)

The truth is that Miriam and Aaron
stood in the office of prophet, and the Lord
is confirming that they could hear from
Him, though only by visions and dreams.
However, God never told them they were
to run the nation, and He proceeds to lay a
bombshell on them in the next verses:

*⁷ My servant Moses is not so, who is
faithful in all mine house.*
*⁸ With him will I speak mouth to
mouth, even apparently, and not in
dark speeches; and the similitude of*

> *the Lord he shall behold: wherefore*
> *then were ye not afraid to speak*
> *against my servant Moses?*
> (Numbers 12:7-8)

God chose Moses for his faithfulness, not his qualifications, and He makes it clear to Miriam and Aaron that Moses was more faithful than they were—in fact, that he is the most faithful man in all Israel.

God says that He will speak to Miriam and Aaron in dreams and visions because of their qualifications (they are prophets), but He will have a face to face relationship with Moses because of his faithfulness.

As a faithful man, Moses thought of the people before himself or his reputation. When the pressure was great against the nation of Israel, Moses put himself on the line for the people. He stood in the gap between God and the sinning nation on more than one occasion.

In contrast, Miriam and Aaron were displaying one of the most obvious attributes of the highly qualified: self-centered arrogance. They were not thinking of the good of the whole nation, nor were they considering Moses' personal fulfillment or right to remarry. They were feeling threatened and were interested only in preserving their personal positions.

As a result, they became guilty of one of the worst sins—slander against God's chosen leadership. I want you to notice that God dealt with this sin publicly.

Not too long after I became pastor of Grace Fellowship, I was approached by a man who told me he could run the church better than I could. I told him I had no doubt he could. He told me he could administrate better than I, and because he had a divinity degree and I did not, he could preach better sermons. Again, I agreed and readily admitted that I had to hire someone to be my administrator.

I looked at this man (whom I found out later had wanted the position of pastor and was angry that he had not been considered), and I told him that there was only one reason I was pastor and he was not: *God called me*. Highly qualified people are usually jealous of the faithful who succeed.

Many of the Psalms of David are written about the qualified who were jealous of David's position and favor with God. He fought jealousy from his brothers, King Saul, members of his own court, and even his own children.

David was nothing more than a faithful shepherd boy who was promoted by the Lord. He made many mistakes while king and committed many sins, but in the end he always repented and rose to the top again. He was just a hayseed who *succeeded*.

The Faithful Love the People

I consider the faithful to be like big corks: you can hold them down for awhile, but they will eventually float back to the top, because they love God and people more than themselves or their reputations.

Moses and David had the same love for the people of Israel that the Lord did. Paul makes the same comment about Timothy:

[19] But I trust in the Lord Jesus to sent Timothy shortly unto you, that I also

*may be of good comfort, when I know
your state.*
[20] *For I have no man like-minted, who
will naturally care for your state.*
[21] *For all seek their own, not the
things which are Jesus Christ's.*
                              (Philippians 2:19-21)

Every minister of the Gospel that Paul
knew, to one degree or another, was pro-
moting himself in the ministry. Timothy
was the only one he knew who did not
have the slightest amount of arrogance or
self-interest. Timothy cared for the Philip-
pian congregation with the same love that
Paul cared for them.

Attributes of the Faithful

What things cause the faithful to succeed? One attribute both Moses and David
had in common was a very meek, or teach-
able, personality. This is something that
cannot be taught; like faithfulness, it is
something that a person must choose.
When confronted with a problem, a meek
person will examine himself first, whereas

a highly qualified person, thinking they cannot make mistakes, will try to blame others.

Another attribute of the faithful person is a reverential fear of the Lord. It is obvious that Miriam and Aaron had no fear of God when they spoke against Moses, God's chosen leader for the nation of Israel. Through their lives, we see that arrogance and jealousy will rob a person of their fear of the Lord, and ultimately lead them into destruction:

> [9] *The anger of the Lord was kindled against them, and he departed.*
> [10] *And the cloud departed from off the tabernacle; and, behold, Miriam became leprous, white as snow and Aaron looked upon Miriam, and, behold, she was leprous.*
>
> (Numbers 12:9-10)

But as we look at the life of Moses, we see that faithfulness and meekness bring a confident respect toward God, and a patient tenderness toward the people. These are the attributes which caused Moses to

ask God to heal Miriam, even though her
sin was directed against him:

> [13] *And Moses cried unto the Lord, say-*
> *ing, heal her now, O God, I beseech*
> *thee.*
> [14] *And the Lord said unto Moses, If*
> *her father hat but spit in her face,*
> *should she not be ashamed seven*
> *days? Let her be shut out from the*
> *camp seven days, and after that let*
> *her be received again.*
>
> (Numbers 12:13-14)

I love what the original Hebrew says
in Proverbs 3:34: God personally sets
Himself in battle array against the arrogant, but He gives grace to the humble. He
defended Moses before the accusations of
Miriam and Aaron, but He granted for-
giveness and healing to Miriam when
Moses requested it.

Six

Elisha's Calling

Again, no matter what type of ministry we have, the principles of success never change—what held true for Moses, David, Paul, and Timothy will hold true for us today. One of the most beautiful examples of calling and separation given to us in the Bible is the story of Elisha the prophet. His life was a tremendous illustration of how faithfulness became the key to the powerful ministry he experienced.

A Man of Passions

In order to understand Elisha's call-ing, we must begin before he comes on the scene, to see what events set the stage for his ministry. His call was based on the failure of the prophet he replaced, Elijah.

James 5:17 tells us that *"Elijah was a man subject to like passions as we are."* The word *passions* is used instead of emo-tions because Elijah had peaks and valleys of emotions far greater than most other men. Elijah was often up and down from minute to minute, rather than day to day.

In the nineteenth chapter of 1 Kings, Elijah has just awakened after an eventful day of calling down fire from heaven, de-stroying four hundred and fifty prophets of Baal, praying for and receiving rain which ended a three-and-a-half-year drought, and outrunning the king's char-iot across the plains of Jezreel.

This morning greets him with a letter from Queen Jezebel that says she intends to cut his throat because he has destroyed all of the prophets of Baal. In weakness and terror, Elijah runs for his life to try to escape.

We are often most vulnerable to a defeat immediately after a great victory, and Elijah's defenses were down. He was obviously not thinking clearly. After all, if the queen were really going to kill him, she would have sent a messenger with a knife, not a letter!

Queen Jezebel was terrified of Elijah, as were the rest of God's enemies, so she tried to frighten him, and it worked. Elijah ran until his strength gave out, and then he collapsed under a juniper tree, crying to the Lord, "I wish I were dead."

Now, Elijah didn't really want to die. If he really wanted to die, he should have stayed in town where Jezebel would have seen to it! He just wanted sympathy. Have you ever wanted somebody to sympathize with you when you were feeling rotten?

I can't tell you how many times I have had someone come to my office, slump down in the chair in front of my desk and say, "I wish I were dead." I know they don't mean it, or they wouldn't have come for help. They could have found many ways to die before they hit my door.

I've often wished I had a gun in my top drawer to pull out on such occasions, slide across the desk, and say, "Go ahead." I would love to see the facial expression that would produce!

But the Lord was more gracious to Elijah. He baked him a cake and gave him water. I don't know what that cake recipe was, but I would like to have it, because Elijah ran on the energy in that cake for forty days and nights. The only problem was that he ran in the wrong direction!

God intended for Elijah to go back to town and continue his ministry. Instead he ran to a cave in Mount Horeb and collapsed again. Again, he wished he were dead and complained that he was the only one who cared for the ministry anymore.

Now we have a much more serious case of "Woe is me." At this point, God is not about to give him sympathy or bake another cake. He tells Elijah to go stand on the mountain, and then He sends a great wind, an earthquake, and finally a fire. Elijah expects these to be supernatural signs. Like most of us, if he didn't get sympathy, a sign or miracle would certainly do!

Elijah is thinking he has God on a string—all he has to do is pull it by pleading his deplorable situation, ask for sympathy, and he can get miracle cakes, earthquakes, winds, and fire. But to his dismay, the Lord was not in any of these.

God spoke to Elijah in a still small voice, one which could not be heard with the ear, and told him to stop looking for guidance in outward signs. By this, God was instructing him to go back to what had made his ministry successful before: the direction of the Holy Spirit.

This was not what Elijah wanted to hear! So he wrapped his mantle around himself and went right back to the mouth of the cave. When God asked him what he was doing there, he repeated his earlier complaint, that he was the only prophet left and no one else cared about the things of God. Again, he was seeking sympathy, and God had had enough.

God is longsuffering, but *not infinitely-suffering*! He informed Elijah that his ministry was about to come to an end, that Elijah was to anoint Elisha of Abel-meholah to stand in his place, and, further, that there were seven thousand in Israel who still had not bowed to Baal!! If Elijah would not lead them, God would anoint someone else.

Elijah and Elisha

When Elijah found Elisha, the young boy was plowing with twelve yoke of oxen, which represented great prosperity in the ancient world. Only the wealthiest had oxen to sacrifice to the Lord. The poor offered turtledoves and pigeons, and the middle class offered rams and lambs. So Elisha, with twelve yoke of oxen, was obviously very prosperous. He was not just a farmer, but a rancher.

As soon as Elijah saw Elisha, he took off his mantle and threw it around the shoulders of Elisha. Not only did Elisha recognize the famous prophet, but he also knew what the mantle represented. He knew immediately that God was *calling* him to stand in the office of prophet and that one day he would take Elijah's place.

This first time that Elijah gives the mantle to Elisha represents his *calling*. Many years later, when the mantle is given the second time as Elijah is taken up to heaven, it marks Elisha's *separation* and the beginning of his ministry.

After Elijah placed the mantle on Elisha in the field, Elisha sacrificed a pair of his oxen and boiled the flesh. He was signifying that he was burning all bridges behind him. He never returned to ranching again, but followed Elijah from that moment.

I want to point out that Elisha was *chosen by God* to stand in Elijah's place. Many believers today think—and some even teach—that ministry offices and spiritual gifts are passed on to those who hang around other ministers and serve them. In some circles it is also taught that offices and gifts are passed on by the laying on of hands.

These are distortions of this story of Elijah and Elisha. You can hang around another minister until you die and never have his anointing, office, or gifts. You can have the most powerful ministers in the world lay their hands on you until the hair is rubbed off your head and never have their anointing.

If you are called by God, association with great men and women of God will bless you, but it will not equip you. The laying on of hands is performed on ministers at the point where God is separating them. It is a ritual in which men recognize what God has already ordained in a minister's life.

Elisha's ministry as he walked with Elijah was far from glamorous. He did not perform any miracles, call down fire, or hold back the rain. He was a servant. He carried Elijah's luggage, found hotel rooms, and probably listened to Elijah complain! And, to my own amazement, Elisha followed Elijah not just a few months, but ten years. How would you like to follow a man like Elijah for ten years?

What did Elisha experience during ten years of ministering to every need and desire of Elijah? Did he sit in the hotel room at night and hear him complain that no one else cared about the ministry but himself? I wonder how many times Elisha heard Elijah say, "I wish I were dead!"

What would you think when the great man of God said, "I wish I were dead?" I suppose Elisha must have been shocked at first. Maybe his whole image of the prophet was shattered. Perhaps more than once he questioned his decision to leave ranching, as he watched Elijah sit on the edge of his bed, feeling sorry for himself.

The Word of God tells us in James that Elijah was a man of passions. We know that ministers are human beings, not angels. Part of every minister's life is knowing, accepting, and dealing with his own and his fellow ministers' imperfections. Elisha must have seen Elijah fail as often as he saw him succeed, but he faithfully served him and respected the office in which his master stood.

There also may have been many anxious moments as Elisha watched Elijah speak to the people and groups of prophets. Elisha had probably studied on his own and put many sermons together, knowing that one day Elijah would turn to him and say, "Elisha, you have the message today, and I want you to give it." But it never happened.

It would be easy to become discouraged over a period of ten years. Elisha must have remembered the day he was called often. He probably rehearsed in his mind over and over again how Elijah threw the mantle over his shoulders, encouraging himself that God, who began the work, would complete it. The God who called him would one day separate him.

So Elisha remained faithful. He plodded on day after day, month after month, and year after year until finally, in 2 Kings 2:1-15, we come to the time of his separation.

Elisha's Separation

And it came to pass, when the Lord
would take up Elijah into heaven
by a whirlwind, that Elijah went
with Elisha from Gilgal.
—2 Kings 2:1

The time for Elijah to be taken was very close. Elisha knew it, but his faithfulness to follow Elijah closely was not based on a greedy desire to have power or an office, but on his character.

For ten years his faithfulness has built a foundation of stability and wisdom. He

has watched Elijah very carefully and
learned many things he should and should
not do. His qualifications had come from
on-the-job training, and the Lord revealed
that the time of separation had arrived:

> [2] *And Elijah said unto Elisha, Tarry*
> *here, I pray thee; for the Lord hath*
> *sent me to Bethel. And Elisha said*
> *unto him, As the Lord liveth, and as*
> *thy soul liveth, I will not leave thee.*
> *So they went down to Bethel.*
>
> (2 Kings 2:2)

It has often been taught that Elisha
stayed with Elijah because he knew he
would receive the double portion if he saw
Elijah go, but this was not even known
until later (v. 10). Elisha followed Elijah
because he was faithful and because he
wanted to learn everything he possibly
could, even during the last hours.

He was not ashamed or too proud to
admit he did not know everything. This is
the downfall of many ministers today.
They do not study, listen to tapes, or take
advice from other ministers, because that

would be admitting there was something they did not know.

However, the wise minister, like Elisha, wants to be around others who know more than he does. (And the longer you live and the more you learn, the more you discover you do not know!)

The Faithful Meets the Qualified

> [3] *And the sons of the prophets that were at Bethel came forth to Elisha, and said unto him, Knowest thou that the Lord will take away thy master from thy head today? And he said, Yea, I know it; hold ye your peace.*
>
> (2 Kings 2:3)

The sons of the prophets here are the *qualified* ones. They had gone to the prophets' school and had degrees on their walls signed by the leading ministers in the land. And, they were all wondering why one of them had not been chosen to take Elijah's place.

They are examples of the *"many* [who] *are called"* (Matthew 22:14), who depend on their qualifications all their lives. But Elisha was *"chosen"* because he was found faithful. The qualified are usually jealous of the faithful.

The fact that Elijah was going to be taken soon was apparently well known by those in the ministry. The sons of the prophets were using their knowledge of this to try to intimidate Elisha. They reminded him that for ten years he had done nothing but watch, as an understudy watches the star, and the time was coming when he would have to stand on his own two feet center stage.

After ten years, Elisha may have become comfortable with his second-in-command position. All of the final decisions had rested on Elijah's shoulders, and the thought of taking ultimate responsibility might have suddenly seemed awesome to him.

"What are you going to do Elisha? Elijah will be gone soon. What are you going to do?" asked the prophets. I like Elisha's reply: "I know it, hold your peace," or, in other words, "Shut up."

Elisha did not know exactly what was going to happen, and he clearly did not like to be reminded of it. More than that, he did not need a chorus of prophets, voicing fear and unbelief, to surround him. So he told them to be quiet. This is another mark of his maturity— he was able to accept and deal with his weaknesses.

Although Elisha did not know what would happen tomorrow, he knew that the God who called him while he was plowing in the fields would know what to do. He would look to God when the time came for him to step into Elijah's shoes.

Tomorrow is often a surprise to us, but never to God, and we do not always need to know the future in order to be successful. The successful minister crosses bridges when he comes to them, whether or not the Holy Spirit shows them to him in advance. After all, where would the walk of faith be if we knew every circumstance we would face?

Our security, and Elisha's security, is rooted and gounded in the knowledge that God knows what tomorrow holds for us, and that He has already prepared a way of escape from—or knows the answer to— any problem we will face.

Elisha faced the sons of the prophets again, approaching him with the same doubts and questions, as he traveled from Bethel to Jericho with Elijah:

> *⁶ And Elijah said unto him; Tarry, I pray thee, here; for the Lord hath sent me to Jordan. And he said, As the Lord liveth, and as thy soul liveth, I will not leave thee. and they two went on.*
> *⁷ And fifty men of the sons of the prophets went, and stood to view afar off and they two stood by Jordan.*
>
> (2 Kings 2:6-7)

As Elijah and Elisha approached the Jordan River, the last place they would be together, the sons of the prophets from Bethel and Jericho stood on the bank of the river and watched from a distance. These men had tried twice to convince Elisha that he was not qualified to take the place of Elijah. Now they stood to the side and waited for him to fail.

To the sons of the prophets, Elisha was the dumb klutz who, though faithful, was naive and uneducated. He had not attended their schools, nor had he asked them for any advice. God knew that they have tried to help him, but Elisha had foolishly turned them down each time. Elisha would ask and learn from those who truly wanted to help him, but was wise enough to avoid the self-righteous, proud, and boastful. Now they were standing by, ready to offer their help when Elisha's great fall came.

The Mantle Is Passed

> [8] *And Elijah took his mantle, and wrapped it together, and smote the waters, and they were divided hither and thither, so that they two went over on dry ground.* (2 Kings 2:8)

This was the last miracle that Elijah performed and would be the first miracle that Elisha performed in his ministry also

(2 Kings 2:14). Elisha took up the same ministry Elijah left and carried on God's call to Israel.

The Jordan River has always represented new beginnings for Israel. This is the same place and the same miracle that God performed when the children of Israel crossed into Canaan in Joshua 3:16. It will also be the place where Jesus will be baptized and separated into his ministry in Matthew 3:13-17. The Jordan River now marks the end of Elijah's ministry and the beginning of Elisha's.

> [9] *And it came to pass, when they were gone over, that Elijah said unto Elisha, Ask what I shall do for thee, before I be taken away from thee. And Elisha said, I pray thee, let a double portion of thy spirit be upon me.*
>
> (2 Kings 2:9)

Elisha's request for a double portion of Elijah's anointing almost sounds prideful. Your first reaction may be like mine—you may imagine that Elisha was thinking something such as: "Bless God, I have been waiting for this moment! I've been traveling with this man for ten years, listening to his complaining and pouting, and if he asks me what I want, I'm going to let him have it with both barrels!"

But Elisha's request was not based on resentment, but Scripture. In Israel, the double portion is the *birthright of the first born son*. Elijah had no family, and Elisha had forsaken his when the mantle was placed on his shoulders at his calling in the fields. Through the years, these two men became like father and son. Elisha was asking for the family inheritance. This same relationship occurred between Paul and Timothy (Philippians 3:22, 1 Timothy 1:2, 2 Timothy 1:2), and it should be noted that Jesus promised a one hundred-fold return in this lifetime for those who would forsake their family for the sake of the Gospel (Matthew 19:29).

> *10 And he said, Thou hast asked a hard thing: nevertheless, if thou see me when I am taken from thee, it shall be so unto thee; but if not, it shall not be so.* (2 Kings 2:10)

The reason that this request was so difficult to grant was not because Elijah did not want to see Elisha have it. It was a hard thing because the anointing was not his to give, but God's. Although the request would be granted, one more test still remained—one more test of faithfulness.

I want you to see that God still was not looking for qualifications, but a renewed commitment and faithfulness to Himself from Elisha. Now that the mantle would be passed to him and the time of separation had arrived, God wanted to know that faithfulness was Elisha's way of life, not just something he walked in to bring him to this point. Also, He knew that a renewed sense of faithfulness rids the soul of any temptation to sit down on acquired qualifications when the ministry begins.

[11] And it came to pass, as they still went on, and talked, that, behold, there appeared a chariot of fire, and horses of fire, and parted them both asunder and Elijah went up by a whirlwind into heaven. (2 Kings 2:11)

Elijah left his ministry as dramatically as he had entered it. Fire was a great symbol for his ministry. Just as he had called it down on the sacrifice on Mount Carmel, God now called fire down to take him home.

The chariot which picked up Elijah was the ***chariot of Israel***, and the horses were driven by angels who were part of the angelic host who protected Israel, bringing divine deliverance when Israel depended on the Lord. They had been there all the time, but now they ***appeared***. Later, when Israel came under tremendous attack, Elisha remembered this glimpse of the heavenly host (2 Kings 6:17). He knew that behind the natural chariots and horses of Israel stood the true defenses of Israel (Psalm 20:7).

[12] *And Elisha saw it, and he cried, My father, my father, the chariot of Israel, and the horsemen thereof. And he saw him no more. And he took hold of his own clothes, and rent them in two pieces.* (2 Kings 2:12)

When the chariot of fire came between Elijah and Elisha, separating them and taking Elijah to heaven, Elisha's first cry was, *"My father, my father!"* Their earthly relationship was over, and the time for the inheritance, the double portion, had come.

As the mantle floated to the ground, Elisha tore his own clothes and prepared to accept his new position. His faithfulness through the years had not only brought him this far, but it constituted the solid foundation and stability which would see him through the course of his ministry.

The time of separation had come. Just as Elisha cut all ties with his past when he was called by slaying the costly oxen, he now ripped his clothing to signify that he was no longer the prophet's servant, but God's chosen prophet to Israel.

Signs and Wonders Shall Follow

13 He took up also the mantle of Elijah that fell from him, and went back, and stood by the bank of Jordan;
14 And he took the mantle of Elijah that fell from him, and smote the

> *waters, and said, Where is the Lord
> God of Elijah? And when he also had
> smitten the waters, they parted hither
> and thither. and Elisha went over.*
>
> (2 Kings 12:13-14)

In these verses of Scripture, we see
how God delivered Elisha, confirming his
ministry and his double portion, but we
also see *why*. Elisha's first question after
the mantle settled upon his shoulders was
"Where is the Lord God of Elijah?" He was
not looking for Elijah's mantle (the position) or Elijah's anointing (the power); but
indeed he was looking for Elijah's God.

True success in ministry comes only
through total and complete dependence on
the Lord. We cannot hang on to old ways
"just in case." There must be a total aban-
donment to the will of God, and no provision for turning back if and when the
going gets tough or we fail in some area.

We can follow in someone's footsteps,
sit at their desk, preach from their notes,
or listen to their tapes—and never have
their power. What we need is not their
notes and tapes, but their God.

When Elisha asked this searching question and hit the same waters which had been divided only moments before, the same God produced the same miracle for him. The personalities of Elijah and Elisha were very different, but their God was the same.

Elijah was strong, outgoing, and bold in front of the heathen. The miracles God performed through him were as spectacular as his life. On the other hand, Elisha was quiet, and though God performed twice as many miracles through him as through Elijah, they were not as grand.

Where Elijah's ministry was primarily before the heathen, Elisha ministered mostly to the house of Israel. He worked with the school of the prophets and did little before the masses of nonbelieving Baal worshippers.

Nevertheless, his God was Elijah's God. His life illustrates that the success of ministry is not in personality, size of building, manner of dress, or model of car you drive. Success in ministry comes from knowing God and moving in His power.

> *15 And when the sons of the prophets which were to view at Jericho saw him, they said, The spirit of Elijah doth rest on Elisha. And they came to meet him, and bowed themselves to the ground before him.* (2 Kings 2:15)

God spoke louder than words and confirmed His choice of Elisha when He parted the waters of the Jordan River. Miracles, signs, and wonders have always been God's stamp of approval on a ministry, and this miracle broke through the critical attitude of the sons of the prophets.

Whether it was Jesus' ministry (Acts 2:22), those who traveled with him (Hebrews 2:4), or our ministry today (Mark 16:17-18), the God of Elijah will produce the miracles of Elijah and cause the critics, scoffers, and mockers to bow. Those who had once opposed Elisha were now for him.

> *7 When a man's ways please the Lord, he maketh even his enemies to be at peace with him.*   (Proverbs 16:7)

Eight

What about Your Ministry?

In the church today, we refer to those whom God calls to be professional ministers as "full-time" ministers. However, being a minister of the Gospel is not something reserved just for those behind the pulpit or on Christian television. Every believer is in the full-time ministry.

God has no part-time help, and believers who run drill presses, wait tables, or sit behind desks are as much in full-time ministry as the pastor of a large church or the evangelist who holds crusades around the world.

So you can see that the secret to success in ministry is not *what* office you stand in, but *who* put you there. Are you in Bible school because it seemed like a good idea at the time, or did God direct you there? Are you an attorney because you can make a good living for your family, or did God call you to the legal profession?

If you are in God's will, you can be as fulfilled, peaceful, and spiritually productive in a workshop as you can behind a pulpit Jesus will not discriminate between "full-time" ministers and ministers in secular positions when He grants rewards at the judgment seat of Christ. The Word of God says that we will all be rewarded based on what we did with whatever He gave us. *"Unto whomsoever much is given, of him shall be much required"* (Luke 12:48).

As a pastor of a church, over the years I have seen many believers zealously desire to move into full-time ministry for the wrong reasons. In most cases, they were led by outward pressures and not by the Spirit of God.

> *14 For as many as are let by the Spirit of God, they are the sons* [mature children] *of God.* (Romans 8:14)

If you are led in your spirit by the Holy Spirit, then you will avoid the following reasons *not* to go into the ministry:

1. **Friends Are in the Ministry**.

Your example for the ministry is not your friends, but the Lord Jesus Himself. "*...but they, measuring themselves by themselves, and comparing themselves among themselves, are not wise*" (2 Corinthians 10:12). As I pointed out in the first chapter, God is the one who created the plan for your life, and He will place friends in your life who will merely *confirm* what He has *already revealed to you* in your heart.

2. **Pressure from a Guest Minister**.

Traveling evangelists or visiting missionaries often see the great needs of the world and take on the role of God's recruiter. Through emotional appeals and stirring slide presentations, they tell you not to wait to be drafted, but to volunteer now for God's army. After all, the Word of God says "go," so you do not have to think or pray about it, but simply go.

All of this can be deceptive, and as a result the world is filled with enthusiastic but quickly frustrated ministers who either were not called to be where they are, or went out too soon and were never separated. Even Jesus was not directed by the needs of the world, but by *the will of God*.

If you minister because of the needs you see, you will spread yourself too thin and quickly become discouraged. However, if you accept your calling and are faithful to do what God leads you to do day by day, you will be content. Then, when you see a need, you can pray for and financially support ministries that God has called to meet that need. This is why the body of Christ is a team and not just one member!

3. You Feel Like You Are Getting Old.

You may have been saved or recommitted your life to the Lord at an older age, and now you feel like you have wasted your life. But the Holy Spirit tells us in Colossians 4:5 that God is *"redeeming the time,"* and He can make up for lost years if you will move at *His* pace. There are many examples in God's Word of those who began a successful ministry later in life. Moses, for instance, entered the ministry at eighty years old.

4. The Ministry Looks Glamorous.

Your job seems dull, and you are only winning a few people to Christ now and then, while the masses in exotic locations around the country and the world are crying for Jesus. The grass always looks greener on the other side of the television set, where thousands are saved as Billy

Graham, Oral Roberts, or some other great man of God preaches the Gospel. The truth is, the ministry is far from glamorous, and the work is very hard. Many full-time ministers would gladly trade places with you at the factory or office, and their families would love for them to have a nine-to-five, Monday-through-Friday job like everyone else.

Your ministry at the office may not always be exciting to you, but it is to the Lord. You and your ministry are just as important to Him as the famous evangelist and his ministry, and He has a specific purpose for you being where you are.

5. **Jesus Is Coming Soon.**

Since the Lord's return could come at any moment, you feel as if you need to be "out there." What if Jesus came and you were not fulfilling your calling?

The fact of the matter is, you cannot fulfill your calling unless you are faithful to what the Lord leads you to do now, for this moment. *"The steps of a righteous man are ordered of the Lord"* (Psalm 37:23). I would rather be found diligently preparing for the ministry when Jesus comes, than to be "out there" too soon with nothing to preach and probably making a mess of my life and the lives of those around me.

God is pleased with those who exercise patience and wait for His timing. Don't be worried that God will overlook or forget you. He knows right where you are and He knows when to separate those whom He has called. What the Lord has begun in you, He will complete.

> [8] *The Lord will perfect that which concerns you.*   (Psalm 138:8)

More than anything, remember that God created you for a reason. He has a plan and a purpose for your life. You are not an accident or an afterthought, and He knows the end of your life from the beginning.

If you will put your trust in the Lord, believe His Word, live it out through the

guidance of the Holy Spirit, and be faithful
to do what He's called you to do, then you
will achieve success in life and great rewards in eternity. More than that, your
life will be pleasing to God, a blessing to
all the lives you touch, and a tremendous
joy for you.

> *⁴ Delight thyself also in the Lord; and*
> *he shall give thee the desires of thine*
> *heart.*
> *⁵ Commit thy way unto the Lord; trust*
> *also in him; and he shall bring it to*
> *pass.*   (Psalm 37:4-5)

About the Author

Bob Yandian is pastor of Grace Fellowship in Tulsa, Oklahoma. His anointed teaching ministry, boldly proclaiming the uncompromised Word of God, is founded on Isaiah 33:6: *"Wisdom and knowledge shall be the stability of thy times, and strength of salvation."*

When he was called to the ministry, Bob left Oklahoma State University to attend Trinity Bible College, whose director and founder, Charles Duncombe, traveled with Smith Wigglesworth. After graduating, he studied Greek at Southwestern College in Oklahoma City.

As a founding member of Grace Fellowship, Bob began teaching various Sunday school classes, one which grew to over 200 in attendance. He was employed by Kenneth Hagin Ministries as Tape Production Manager in 1973, and this led to his becoming an instructor at Rhema Bible Training Center in 1977. Soon after that, he was appointed Dean of Instructors at Rhema, but resigned in 1980 to become Pastor of Grace Fellowship. Under his leadership the church has grown from 1,200 to 3,000.

Bob not only ministers the Word of God to his congregation, but he also teaches at Grace Fellowship's School of the Local Church and hosts his annual Pastors' Conference every January. He and his wife Loretta live in Tulsa with their two children, Lori and Robb.